Children of Someone Else's Longing

"'She sculpts the sand with her name in humongous letter' could easily be a description of poetry written by Sandra Rokoff-Lizut. The author guides her readers through landscapes of youth and innocence, past the divisions of a world and family stripped to essentials, and then gently deposits us on the shores of old age and unstoppable change. Every reader, no matter the stage of life they currently inhabit, will find connection and meaning in this collection of poems."

— Susan Shumway, co-member of poetry group, "Poetic License"

"Sandra Rokoff-Lizut launches the reader into a world of uncertainty with the title to her new collection of poetry, *Children of Someone Else's Longing*. She moves back in time to capture the dark and the lightness of her childhood where a young girl dreams of skating so her "silver blades spit shavings;" where, as a fifteen-year-old, she tucks her spirit into a tree, too unwieldy to carry in the "heavy backpack" that is the body; wherein a dream a "fox-like creature is gnawing at her hair;" and where, In "The Way a Marriage Ends," her cheating husband unscrews the lightbulb from the overhead lamp on his way out the door. In her world, the death of hope releases her to "a course not contemplated."

Her memories "rush down" to greet her, time stopping only for her grandchildren. Rokoff-Lizut memorializes and celebrates the continuation of her line. No idealizations, her gaze is unflinching, her anxieties laid bare. Rokoff-Lizut gives us an apt portrayal of our time where uncertainty is the new normal. Her poems also include her fears for the future of the planet, a theme that weaves seamlessly with her observations of nature. 'What if we would put the world back tree by tree—' Hope is not entirely defeated."

— Rachel Barton, Editor, *Willawaw Journal*

"The pictures of individuals evoked in this collection of Sandra Rokoff-Lizut's poetry are extraordinarily well-crafted from her life experiences, expressed with deep understanding of human nature. They come from her heart, and some are stories of people in her life expressed with empathy, sadness, humor, and wit. Some are expressed with poignant sadness about the oppression endured by those without white privilege. Some are evoked by her thoughts about public figures.

As someone who has been a close friend for years I know that these written pictures will also be enjoyed by the reader, who will appreciate the reflections about imperfect parents, the joy of children and grandchildren, and aging. The collection includes a wide range of topics, from very personal memories of the sometimes horrors of babysitting, being not Jewish and marrying a Jew, enjoying children, grandchildren, and a loving second marriage, to reflections on politics, diversity, and odes to poets. Sandy writes from old memories and new experiences. When she visited a tribal community with me her response was to write a heartfelt comment on resilience in spite of overwhelming losses."

— Jane Latané, aspiring poet and semi-retired educator

Children of Someone Else's Longing

Sandra Rokoff-Lizut

Apprentice
House Press
Loyola University Maryland

First Edition

Paperback ISBN: 978-1-62720-407-1
Ebook ISBN: 978-1-62720-408-8

Printed in the United States of America

Design by: Katie McDonnell
Edited by Meghan O'Hora
Promotion plan by Amber Davis

Published by Apprentice House Press

Apprentice
House Press
Loyola University Maryland

Apprentice House Press
Loyola University Maryland
4501 N. Charles Street
Baltimore, MD 21210
410.617.5265
www.ApprenticeHouse.com
info@ApprenticeHouse.com

Contents

To My husband Roger
for his valuable suggestions
and emotional support

We

        are all ancestors

of the future // tucked

                into musty
                pages of // the past

        all dreams

of // the past
      hidden   in // tiny crevices of
                      someone else's longing

        all children of
     someone else's longing

                though we don't know whose

****

Cathedral

I encountered
a potato tabernacle
                              hewn in rock
            beneath   a red madrone.

A soundless
                        sacred place.
                                    Lichen-covered
cave.

Sunshine streamed // sweet citrus   through its seams.

I loved to // tiptoe
                    s l o w l y // round
                                        that church
of mine.

Toe-taps clicked
like abacus ticks.
                        Outstretched arms // preparing to float
free.

I'm not only flooded   with such memories
                                        now // I hear

more rushing // down
the hill   to greet me // greenly.

Turning Ten Today

— for Sylvie

She sculpts the sand   with her name

                                                     in

humongous // letters

handstands with // abandon

                            cartwheels with \/ \/ \/ \/

unbounded joy.

Tides & time
will claim
the name   written on the shore

mark a million cycles

                     of /\ /\ cartwheels heading \/

                                     toward a future.

But now her head // points down

                            both legs rise in a perfect V

toes aim for the sun

                     & time holds its breath.

Ella Watson

— *Chairwoman for a federal agency, photographed by Gordon Parks, Washington, DC, 1942. The picture became a symbol of the pre-civil*
— *rights era's treatment of minorities.*

Chosen for her
color // sex // station.
A symbol. Posed
before her nation's
flag, she stiffly // stands
to have her picture taken
flanked by cleaning tools.

Thin. Dressed in faded
calico // pins in places
fasteners should go. Two
plastic buttons still // large
// round // brightly
white. In the center
at her waist, they trap
& bind her tight.

Note how the bodice
drapes across the flatness
of // her chest. Was this
once another's frock,
used // then tossed
or given by
a stranger
more abundantly
endowed?

A small hole // appears below
the waist where // handles
of her mop & broom
have pressed into the cloth

// flesh a smidgen
every minute
every second
of every day.

The culprits // both
broom & mop //
propped up at her
front & side so
we can view
their wear // the dirt
the bend of tired bristles
the slug-like // filthy
strings.

A huge flag
hangs behind her
in a vertical display.
Old Glory,
with its // field
of stars // sends stripes
of blood & purity
downstream,
behind her back.

Here she is:
an icon // woman
asked to pose. Smooth
oval face reads // *placid*.
Curly grayish hair forced flat.
Eyeglass frames a little
bit askew. She tucks
her chin // pulls herself
away
            from
                 us.

Deliver Us from Evil

He whirls her away from girlhood & kin.
Coiled tightly round his body, like the snake
inked on his arm, she blooms // for a moment.

Thick haze grows around her, almost protects
from his crazy // from his mean. But when he's out,
her world inside the dirty cracked windows shrinks.
And now the infant, with little sour milk smells,
downy crown // mewling.

Summer of salvation // he repents,
sways & prays in giant tents.
Rants about *The Rapture*.

Summer of perdition // she pretends.
Cowed & confused // in sweaty dreams
she fights attacking raptors.

He drives her toward *Deliverance* in a borrowed car,
speeding across desert highways with a thirst greater
than the one he has for water. She
withers beside him.

At a rest stop in Oregon
he smokes & drinks free coffee.
She props the child against a stone
on soft piney needles // inhales smells
of sunlight & decay.

Talons extend
massive wings beat // block sun.

Tiny arms reach toward heaven.

Initiation Dream

She wades   thigh-high   in tide pools   through
                                                        stones // shells
                                                        simple
                                                        sea creatures.
Below
a flat-headed
fox-like
creature
wraps round
a rock beneath
the water;   land // animal   living
submerged.

She makes // eye
contact knowing she's
doing // a forbidden
thing. The beast   springs up her back //
clawing   gnawing at her // hair.

As she
struggles
to break
free // people   circle // guarded //
hesitant   reluctant // to help.

Then // a stranger

calmly // disentangles   the beast,

carefully wraps   it in soft   fabric & returns
it,

like borrowed treasure   to its
place   by the rock // below.

She stands
dumbfounded
shaken // yet
not
broken.   Abando
ning the beach
she wanders
under moss-laden
                                  trees where // unbeknownst,

countless offspring
of the strange
creature //   lark about in the branches.

Sweet babe of the bayou

                        strangled
by kudzu,
bound by fine   flounces
slips // out of her life.

Sinks down // through
the boggy
                    this child of our past,
                    into the realm // of
                    the zombies // where

children like her
once rosy with

                            virtue & flaxen with
                            good // rise up with
                            weapons & mouths

full of // hate.

Now undead in
the bayou // crown   circled with kudzu

she swipes her white frock
                    with blood from a knife.

Definitions // Hope

slowly

                             flickers till its last bit
                                 of strength is spent

We are then released
to mourn

                             released to heal

released to stumble
upon a course
not contemplated

                             before hope
                             blocked our entry

Pink Seesaws

— *July /2019: Two artists built three temporary seesaws across the U.S.-Mexico border.*

Particles of
            lightheartedness

they do
still exist
you know

float & bind together

into   rosy   horizontal lines,

settle into structures we used to call
            teeter-totters.

A tiny pink playground cuts
through nasty
barriers;   beckoning children.

A child in Mexico
touches the sky,   a child in
the US touches

the ground; then they
                trade.

Languages different;

            laughter   the same.

On Pollywog Pond

The young girl's

ankles bend to   greet each other.

Red nose
drips   colt-legs wobble

mittened hands
        pose
        to hold
ice at bay.

Lips & cheeks
chap. Toes   lose ability to twinkle.

But in her
mind she   glides
          spins
          jumps
          stops
          so fast

silver blades spit shavings.

As Oregon winter begins

autumn weeps
its last leaves
on dark dank
afternoons

limbs
bravely bare
their vulnerability

grey sheets
unravel
in an un-
failing cacophony
of rain drops

Infested House

I remember the bad breath
// smell of that clapboard   house above the Hudson
                                              striking me every time

I babysat that winter,
                        a combo of mold // soiled
                        diapers & sickly sweetness

of over-ripe fruit.
                    I hated fixing food there // grimy stove
                    // jelly-gobbed counters. So, I opened
                    cans of Spaghetti-O's that night // before
                    reading the twins *two* chapters

of *Doctor Doolittle.*

After powdering & changing   the baby // tucking all three
                                        into bed & starting back
                                        down the scruffy staircase,

I saw the first one // creeping
across a toy-strewn carpet. *Cat?*
// They didn't have one. Long
hairless tail on a body   the size of a newborn!

I ran back upstairs //   shut myself in the baby's
                                    room, sat on the floor // back
                                    to the wall // shaking &

rehearsing how to tell

the children's mom.

But she wasn't first home
that night. The sound of her //
husband fumbling keys at

the front door brought me //
downstairs. Leaving the children
unattended, he drove me home //
looking more at me // than the road.

Sandra Dee, he called me, suggesting a
short *sabbatical* at the beach next summer
for // his kids // himself //   & me!

My mind kept busy twisting
the unfamiliar word *sabbatical*   round in my head // while

my hands twisted a gold
& pearl ring (eighth grade
graduation gift from my Dad)   round my finger. It took
                                                                me over a week to
                                                                to call his wife because

I was so embarrassed
to tell her there were //   rats living in
her home.

The Way the Marriage Ends

He unscrews
the light bulb

        from the overhead

lamp
in their
bedroom   & takes it with him

says
he plans

        to live

with a girl
whose name
he'd mentioned

        one time
           in passing

tells
the children too

        huddled together
        against the
        front door
        promises

           This is a good thing.

The Way It Is Now

— *February 2016: In response to Presidential primary debates*

as I nap
through
unquiet
afternoons

the world
too // dreams
itself away
this din

of rasping
deceptions
grisly // promises
with grasping

meaty hands

Body Language

Does it not seem
possible, that between
his blank page
face & casualness
implied by

pocketing his free
left hand,

the officer gives
us an impression
of shunning
his own humanity;

as his left
knee genuflects
on George Floyd's

neck,
stifling a life
akin to his own?

Icon for The Plight of Her Kind

*In 1936, in the midst of the Great Depression, photographer Dorothea Lange
took a photo for the Resettlement Administration that would become
one of the most iconic images of that time in US history.*

I'll never forget
the moment I shot // that image
two tattered children // faces turned away
naked necks exposed to the camera
leaning on // framing the mother
seated on an old folding chair
in a migrant tent.

Her features faced me // but the gaze
was off-center // guarded
almost absent
thin worn & faded like the fabric
of her clothes // lines etched deep
years too early.

One elbow rested on her knee
hand raised // fingers lingered against her
own cheek rather than that
of the pallid // infant draped across her lap.
Four more kids // somewhere
kids she bore // she tended // she fed.

I took five photos of her that day
& knew the last one harbored
some larger reality // one that
would seize the public's sensibilities
& aid the destitute pea pickers.

That photograph has been
reproduced thousands of times
shown // in museums
& the cover of *Look Magazine.*

I wonder if she had anyone then
husband // a man. I didn't ask many
questions that day // just if I could
take her picture // told her our project
would help people like her.

Florence // I think.

They Fell Like Rain

*— China 1958: as part of the Great Leap Forward campaign to preserve
grain by destroying pests, four million sparrows were killed. Two years
later, when locusts invaded, thirty million people starved to death.*

A peoples' farm collective in a country
rich with jade is the setting for this picture:
        an unsettling act of war. The multitude
            of peasants (who are absent
from this scene) toil endlessly in umber fields
         of grain: tilling, hoeing, picking, packing
            bags of treasure; sacks of precious rice.

In the background of the painting, strung
all across the scene, tree-sized heaps
        resembling hills lifeless
           lumps of clay. With deft
exquisite brush strokes, hues of black
        & blue, the artist has depicted hills
           of dead & dying birds.

Children in the foreground
armed with dim grey pots & pans,
        caught banging clanging
           running wildly
in a screaming screeching frenzy,
        chasing sparrows, breaking eggs,
           destroying pests for Chairman Mao.

Pigtails drooping, one small child looks out from
darkly solemn eyes, with hands outstretched,
      her body bent above that of a dying bird.
But, on her shoulder, firmly planted,
        an older sibling's grim command:

Continue with the task at hand!

Our Mother

The earth does not belong to us. We belong to the earth.
            — *Chief Seattle*

does she want us

did she ever // or will

            she weary // of our silliness

      & shake

                  us from
                              her noble // cloak

                        like vexing // flecks of lint

Tree by Tree // A Triolet

If we would put
the world back

        tree by tree,

   (yes, we can do that; when we really care).

If we would put
the world back

        tree by tree:

   (a billion saplings, mounting majesty)

could mend
the earth,

    (now scraped & raped & bare),

& heal
our own hearts;

     (quaking with despair).

If we would put
the world back

        tree by tree,

   (yes, we can do that when we really care).

We Are Children of an Indifferent Universe

In Oregon City you could
once get twenty cents
for a sea lion's ear & a dollar
for the animal's scalp.

Today, I see four old ladies
kayak near a pair, who's big
bulbous bodies are parked on a pier
barking up at a graying sky.

Some of them endangered now.

Tohono O'odham Tribe
The name "Tohono O'odham" means "People of the Desert."

Winds weave   bits of desert dirt
                & grit
through endless   warps of cobalt blue.

Cactus spines   flaunt plastic bags.

Broken glass

                & beer cans

                        ribbon highways.

Cows & dogs   dodge cars & trucks.

Patrol vans roundup people

                        crossing borders.

    And **still** the *Desert People*

    Dance in Celebration.

As They Head North

Poverty pushes
      scratched
      dented hearts,
     fractured *familias*
as they head north.

Sun-scorched
      feet blistered
      bloodied
      clutching *los ninos,*
 they head north

Danger
      deception
      death,
      eager predators, stalk.
  Head north.

Salvation's
      cruel
      sweet
      siren-call beckons.
North.

Very Old Men with Enormous Wings

— Gabriel Garcia Marquez 1927-2014

This time

when rain   knocked the angel down

he came // looked

took the man's aged hand
veined with
a million magical
words & together
they rose.

Two very old men with enormous wings.

Definitions // Time

the lover   lures us back

into bliss
bids us
                            live there forever.

            *

the thief, filches
                        our youth
& that
of our   children.

            *

the parent, drags us
forward;   snotty-nosed
                           & blubbering.

            *

the elephant
                     staggers round
                        & round

tethers us
                     to today's

minutia

The White Deer

The white deer hangs
      out in a bleak
      spot // desolate

             field // behind
             a deserted *chop shop*
             across the highway

from the // fern-filled
forest where she
sleeps at night.

             In winter's early
             dusks // I purposely
             pass that place &

slow my car to focus.
If I see her // euphoria
dances
        through
            my veins.

My Spirit

to keep it safe
for a while
I stash my spirit
in the crook

of a sycamore tree
as my ancestors
did // because
now that I'm

fifteen my
spirit // is
growing too
wild & unwieldy

for me to carry
around in this
heavy backpack
anymore

¤

Double-Sided Mirror

— Tony Hoagland, *The Question*

they hang there
in the mind
           questions
to which
we have
no answers

                    suspended
                    all around them
                              answers
                    to the questions
                    we were
                    never asked

¤

Moon and Almond Blossoms

The moon hangs heavy on the horizon,

I wish you could recall it too.

Bright & overripe, it rises up & rests
on a thousand pink-white blooming almond trees.

We were young then
living in the hills above the
sea.

Huge moon & the blooms;
dark gypsy caves line a winding roadway to the coast.

On a night like that
how could we not
walk all the way across
the island of Majorca?

Moon bright as filtered sun, enchants, supplies
a compass for our carefree ramble. Miles of tile-
roofed houses planted on the hillside. Fences
made of artichokes. Burros in the road.

We crest the final hill at sunrise,
find a tiny coastal town,

You'd remember its name, I'm sure.

sit with bread & coffee tending very tired feet.

Did it really happen?
(so magical a time)

You were the only other one who knew.

Beneath Blue Hydrangeas

                    In the basement
of the towering Victorian
with peeling paint, an ancient
furnace belches;   startles a small
mouse   encircling it.

Sputtering & spitting,
the great behemoth
strains to face
another winter.

You're right Marie; damn thing's gonna' blow up any minute,
                    jokes man
                    in the top floor
                    apartment.

          Maybe today's the day this place will explode!
                    Young bride, in the lower
                    floor flat   giggles in her
                    husband's ear.

                    I'll save you, sweet pea,
                    he whispers back.

  Outside, a small
                    girl,   playing safely
                    in her nest beneath rusty

blue hydrangeas, hears
the clamor.
Mind filling
                    with fearful thoughts & heart
                    pounding; the child scrambles
                    to her knees.   To save the lives

of her parents & the young
couple who live downstairs;

she presses small
palms together.

In Grandma's Kitchen, 1944

sunlight splashes
worn linoleum
warming morning
toes like cinnamon toast

scrubbed combed
& matching
we sisters plant
obligatory
kisses & harvest
ginger cookies

wooden-shoed
Dutch girls
clomp silently
across kitchen
cabinet doors
on glossy decals

Swiss-cheeked
children circle
Grandma's
aproned girth
(anticipating apples
I think)

blue & white checked
curtains billow
blithely
while a fly
trapped between
glass & screen
soundlessly
screams

Queen Anne's Lace

— in memory of Pam

Beyond houses bound
by planted blooms, the terrain
teems with thistles, milkweed,
a wild blackberry patch. It was

Pam's world, where brambles
& thickets often thwarted
her efforts to gather bounty
& overgrew parts of her path.

But poppies, daisies & sky
blue flax also grace the field.

Snowy flowers too, named
for a Queen who long ago
pricked her finger while
making lace. It's said a drop of
blood falling on her intricate
pattern, lingers still in the heart
of each wild white bloom
where Pam still lives.

Now

Cocooned
deep in stripes of black
& white softness, I sip fine syrah;
tongue seeking promised hints of dried
herbs & fresh violets. Head tilted
back on brightly stitched pillows
from Oaxaca; I bask.

Cross-legged on nearby
rug, my granddaughter
(who is seven),
gently pats blue-gray rabbit
(who is real);
reads him a story she's written
about another rabbit
(who is make-believe).

From the kitchen,
seductive smells
(black beans & sausage)
vie for airspace with
mysterious mathematical
words floating around
our ancient Formica table
by a grandfather doing
homework with a tween.

Outside small square-paned
windows, ruby-tipped vine maples
hold me captive. Touched by
tender breezes in autumn's
early dusk, they slowly
& rhythmically wave
goodbye.

Summer's End

In another week
in another place

a whip-poor-will
will clasp last flecks

of summer in its beak
masticate & savor

its sweet-scented feast
one more last time

Kukui Dream

— *Homage to my son & his Hawaii home*

At sun's first
yawn, he lifts   the tent flap

devouring the island's
aroma &   doles out
                    Costco bird feed.

Beneath the wide
          kukui tree, lava rocks

blanketed with tiny
          doves, pulsate.   Saffron
          finches swoop
                    through
                              droves of puffin-faced
                              sparrows. A crimson

 cardinal   sweeps
                              into the melodious mix.

The young man stands
silently, for one
                    moment, or perhaps,   an eternity,

arms spread wide   like his tree.

                    Overwhelmed by gratitude.

Crabbing

Crack & pick. Suck those skinny
claw shells, glean each tiny morsel,
every succulent speck. My mother
craves the flavor of crabmeat.

Even in land-bound New Mexico
she fishes for eateries offering
Crab Entrée deals for my monthly
visits from Santa Fe,
two young boys in tow.

She & the kids are euphoric. I'm
a bit crabby as I drive us, whiplashed
by winter winds, to god-forsaken
places up the canyon & cockroach-ridden
downtown dives she's only read about.

Mom's been gone now for thirty-odd
Decembers. My sons live in Oregon
& together take an annual crabbing
excursion to the coast.

I picture them there, *cracking & picking.*
They suck those skinny claw shells
gleaning each tiny morsel, every
succulent speck, while unseen beside
them, their grandmother sits
                    licking her lips.

Barbizon Nightgowns

Christmas 1949: the soft whisper
of white tissue paper makes my
nine-year-old heart shiver
as I carefully unveil

my annual favorite gift
(always from Aunt Margaret)
who'd probably wrapped the pink
blue or white fine cotton night-dress

with just a touch of tiny rosebuds
embroidered round the neckline,
while sitting at her polished pecan
writing desk set in deep rose carpet,

surrounded by the safe & sound
smell of my uncle's Jack's pipe,
in the living room of a house
with a built-in wooden breakfast nook,

& backyard like something from
a Wes Anderson *Adirondack Fantasy*
on a street blessed by shade of a hundred
maples & unending swaths of emerald green.

A decade later my mother tells me
that I'll never be able to live there,
(not for lack of financial ability)
but, because of the man I had just married?
A Jew

Zeke In Metaphor

— homage to Sylvia Plath's "Metaphors"

He was a crossword
enigma

              big man in butcher's apron.

Irish bar room ballad

              artichoke in a jelly jar.

Oh, marzipan
nectarine
crate-cradled
in fake grass,

              too lovingly

sculpted to fulfill
your function.

Money escaped

              the confines of his talents.

He was tipped
& emptied
too early.

              Prior to the temperature
              (just below boiling)

that ensures great tea.

Traveling North from Ashland

low-lying
ribbons of fog
circle the mountain
settle at its base
freeing treetops
a piney island
appears

now & again
a certain image
scent whisper
surrounds me
loosens knots
of routine & I
too float free

Baltic Cruise

We are not in immediate danger.

The Captain's static
pushes through dark turbulence
as The Black Sea's icy claws scrape
fourteen chairs from his seventh-story deck.

Waves gnash portholes. Stateroom's sea-saw.
Voyagers stagger through hallways & lounges
searching solutions
for queasy stomachs & quivering hearts.

Waters recede. A collective sigh glides across airwaves
as stability seats itself on the remaining deck chairs,
while in topsy-turvy staterooms, passengers
pick up & sort scattered possessions.

Then, staircases & elevators buzz with animated banter
as the shaky ones regain balance & make their way up
to the eleventh-story deck for today's scheduled tutorial:

Folding Linen Napkin Swans.

They All Gave Me Diamonds

Once for love // once for sex // once for security

Men are like busses
when one leaves

another // shows
up in about twenty minutes.

But diamonds // I love 'em!

These hands are too
old & ugly for them
now // I married three
times & they all gave me diamonds.

Spoken by a woman soon to become
    my
        mother-in-law // as six diamond rings tumble
            from a black velvet pouch

clink on a small cigarette stained
      tabletop
          in the drape-drawn
              Howard Johnson Motel room
       where I meet her
            for the first time.

As thin slivers of New
Mexico sunshine slip through
the space // where shoddy curtains
don't quite meet // the diamonds & I

            blink.

Anniversary

a hotel room
somewhere in
southern Oregon

drizzly dreary
Tuesday afternoon
sometime after two

a couple
on the slippery
side of sixty

sip champagne
indulge in dark
chocolate filled truffles
& giggle

time temporarily
stops takes
a few steps back
dances out the door

Palindrome for Robin Williams

laughter without end
lightning-like wit

heart humongous
ignited humor

mind uneasy
stirred agony & angst

                  angst & agony stirred
                  uneasy mind

                  humor ignited
                  humongous heart

                  wit like lightning
                  end without laughter

What She Wants from Me

Your breath offends
me, as in; *Did you have onions
for lunch, dear?* My dying

mother spits her final spoken
words at me, from a vast

recess of what I consider
judgment; as in the kind
of loving that
wants a child to be
other than they are.

I, first daughter: grown,
wed,   then not wed,   mother of
two small boys, stand
at the head
of my mother's metal bed
attempting to gently blot
present pain, old
anguish & fear,
from her fragile
forehead. On hearing

her question,   I lift my fingers
from the chalky
skin & freeze,   unable

to respond.   Eons pass.
Thoughts unravel.   Words break free.   *Yes, I had chili.*

As usual, in our lives
together, I answer
her question literally;

deaf to her real request.

Mom's Final Gift

The surgeon softly murmurs that
I'll doubtless live a day or so
& tells my two grown daughters
to leave & get some rest.

> *I'm busy dying faster.*

I've willed my remains to science.

> *I can't stand phony '*
> *"'funeral flowers."*

Vodka & V8 in the fridge
so the old dames next door can
go over & drink a final toast.

> *I'm willing my body to close down.*

Rent on the apartment
due in two days' time. If
my girls get a move on, they can
clean the whole place out by then.

> *When the girls leave the hospital*
> *to get some rest, I'll just*
> *wrap up my soul*
> *&*
> *slip out.*

On Turning 80

I cringe, anticipating a watershed birthday,
a hairpin turn I'll suddenly enter
before beginning a dark downward journey.
Then, way too quickly, the day arrives.

With no other option, I breathe deeply
&, with the steadfast moon to guide me,
move cautiously forward.

I'm stunned to find roads ahead much like former ones:
some divided, others potholed
or almost washed away,

some nearly vertical, without guardrails,
others freshly paved with promise
& painted yellow lines.

So, I'll breathe more easily now & travel on
with all of you; our vehicles of differing ages,
makes & conditions, heading, *some of us
more carefully than other*s, all in the same direction.

Knowing, the steadfast moon will follow.

Winter Moons

"At night, the ice weasels come."
   — Matt Groening, "Life in Hell"

Winter's New Moon
conceals ice weasels
crisscrossing whitened
landscapes to convene
sharp teeth
      & claws ready

Winter's Crescent Moon
extends long slim fingers
pulls us trembling
      from warm beds

Winter's Half Moon
holds forth silver vials
of healing potions
begs us to restore
      our faith

Winter's Grandmother
Moon safeguards
swaddles us
in her luminous cloak
then slowly
      turns away again

My aging arms

grasp greedily
    for more
tomorrows. Yet,
yearn to greet
them in
                yesterday's frocks;
                brighter & tighter

than the loose
beige linen
I wear & no
longer attempt   to iron.

Its wide sleeves
hide my grandmother's
ghost; her braided crown
white, like tiny
                buttons on her navy
                dress. In leather

lace-ups & rolled
stockings, Grandma
puffs her *Camels,*
relishing airwaves of
                intrigue & anguish:

Stella Dallas Backstage Wife;
 while cozily tucked
inside folds of my
                crepey upper arms.

On My Son Alexander's Last Day in Paris

                              I watch him study at the Louvre,
stride along the Seine,
lose him at the Place De Ville,
catch his scent again.

                     I creep behind with panther's grace
& silent skulking skill

                    J'espere to trap, recapture him,

(yet know I never will).

                       His youth retreating evermore,
craft & gifts well honed,
he grasps his future hungrily
& gnaws it to the bone.

                    As Paris, softly feather grey,
  enfolds him
          one last time today.

Once They've Left Home

Tucked beneath their beds,
I see their shoes, worn through.

They must climb down
trellises through the nights

under earth's crust to dance,
retrieve rubies & pearls.

Trembles. Wobbles. Falls.
Ascending again,

toes bloodied.
I remember those rungs,

can still feel the unstable footholds.
The truth comes creeping up on me.

Now I hear the crow's call.

Again, I Turn Toward You

Your pearl earrings
still in place,
red slashed   across wrinkled lips,

translucent face   pieces of eggshell
                                              pasted together.

A brisk breeze would disperse you.

I clutch my gut   struggle to breathe.

You died & willed
your body to science
thirty years ago!

Not really dear   *I'll live one more year*
(somewhere in your town)

                                              housebound & needing
                                              lots of care.

She extends a scrap
of paper
to me, I
crumble
the note
containing   her address & phone number,

jam it into
my pocket

        hoping never to find it again.

Farewells

This morning I learn that yet another one
who was part of my life for a time,
many years ago, left her body, lifted her essence
into its own waiting boat & set sail
on the flotilla of souls.

As I grow older now, their leagues increase.
With each exodus I stand for a time
silently on the shore,
waving through a low-hanging cloud of yesterdays,
then walk back home a little slower.

I Am From Sawdust & Snow

I am from sawdust,
       from Rheingold Beer
       & Post Toasties.

I'm from an ancient furnace. Defeated // smelling of fear,
I'm from thick blue hydrangea bushes to hide beneath,
       & many litters of seven-toed kittens
       living in a cardboard jungle behind Zeke's Delicatessen.

       From Thanksgiving at Grandma's.
       From the soft brown Kocher eyes.
       From Zeke & Marie & Uncle John.

I am from the annual play // Mona & I
       pilgrims & pretty little Cousin Joanie // the turkey.
       Later those evenings, I had to put Joanie to bed
       in that ghost-ridden room at the foot of the attic stairs.

I'm from *For god's sake, John & Let's face it girls, you'll*
       never be….
I'm from the church that met over the fire station, never
       comprehending the *Holy Ghost.*
       From Piermont, kale & liver & Neapolitan ice cream.
I'm from the time Uncle John broke his leg in the snow & Marie
       told him not to complain // he'd probably meet & marry
       a nice nurse at Good Samaritan.

       From Aunt Anne, the nurse who married him &
       baked the most beautiful pies.
       From family pictures that disappeared in my mother's
       move to New Mexico fifty years ago.
I am from being a seventy-six-year-old woman, sitting on a bed
       writing poems with enough material supplied by angry,
       alcoholic, funny, colorful, unique, story-telling relatives,
       to last the rest of my life.

POSTSCRIPT

Murmuration

Twilight   ///////
                  a giant wave of
                           starlings swoop   //////
                                     in unison

murrrrrrrrrrrrrr

                                 pattern unlocks
                       separates   unites\\\
\\\
                      undulates in
      opposite directions   \\\\\\\

murrrrrrrrrrrrr

 flocks meet again   ////
               pattern twists \\\\\
                     turns   ////
                         winds
together   /\\\\\\\\\\ faultlessly

                            seamlessly
////////\\\\\
                 murrrrrrrrrrrrrrrrrrrr   dusky
sky /////////   vibrates////////
                   swells /////
             ///   //////// with
swarm intelligence

                rrrrrrrrrrrrrrrrrrrrrrrrrrrrrrrrrrrrrrrr

         Oh, would it be so // for *our* world!

About the Author

Sandra Rokoff-Lizut sees herself as continuously learning, emerging, and striving to offer an authentic, fresh, strong voice to poetry, which she began to study seriously ten years ago at the age of seventy-one. She feels honored to have received an Oregon Poetry Association First Place Award and two honorable mentions. Her poems have appeared in publications that include: *Verses, Illya's Honey, The Penwood Review, Red River Review, Willawaw Journal*, and *The Inflectionist Review*. She resides in Oregon with her husband and three cats.

Acknowledgments

The author extends her heartfelt gratitude to the following journals for previously publishing poems, some in different versions, in *Children of Someone Else's Longing*:

Analekta Anthology: Definitions and Baltic Cruise
Blue Lake Review: Winter Moons
Clackamas Literary Review: Traveling North from Ashland
The Henniker Review: We and Queen Anne's Lace
Illya's Honey: On My Son Alexander's Last Day in Paris and Once They've Left Home
The Inflectionist Review: Turning Ten Today
Jellyfish Whispers: My Spirit
Paper Gardens: The White Deer and In Grandma's Kitchen, 1944
The Penwood Review: Zeke in Metaphor
Red River Review: They All Gave Me Diamonds
The Sacred Cow: Mom's Final Gift
Third Wednesday: Moon and Almond Blossoms
The Tower Journal: The Way the Marriage Ends and Now
Verse Weavers: Barbizon Nightgowns and Very Old Man with Enormous Wings (Winner, 2014 Oregon Poetry Association Contest)
Wilderness House Review: Deliver Us from Evil, Initiation Dream, and Murmuration
Wild Goose Poetry Review: They Fell Like Rain
The Writing Disorder: As Oregon winter begins and On Pollywog Pond

And a very special thanks to the judges of the Oregon Poetry Association for awarding "Very Old Man with Enormous Wings" 1st place and "Palindrome for Robin Williams" honorable mention in their annual poetry contest.

Finally, the author expresses ongoing gratitude to her family, friends, fellow poets, poetry teachers, and especially mentor/agent, John Sibley Williams, for continued encouragement and support of her work.

Apprentice House Press
Loyola University Maryland

Apprentice House is the country's only campus-based, student-staffed book publishing company. Directed by professors and industry professionals, it is a nonprofit activity of the Communication Department at Loyola University Maryland.

Using state-of-the-art technology and an experiential learning model of education, Apprentice House publishes books in untraditional ways. This dual responsibility as publishers and educators creates an unprecedented collaborative environment among faculty and students, while teaching tomorrow's editors, designers, and marketers.

Outside of class, progress on book projects is carried forth by the AH Book Publishing Club, a co-curricular campus organization supported by Loyola University Maryland's Office of Student Activities.

Eclectic and provocative, Apprentice House titles intend to entertain as well as spark dialogue on a variety of topics. Financial contributions to sustain the press's work are welcomed. Contributions are tax deductible to the fullest extent allowed by the IRS.

To learn more about Apprentice House books or to obtain submission guidelines, please visit www.apprenticehouse.com.

Apprentice House
Communication Department
Loyola University Maryland
4501 N. Charles Street
Baltimore, MD 21210
410-617-5265
info@apprenticehouse.com•www.apprenticehouse.com